GREAT MINDS OF SCIENCE

GEORGE WASHINGTON CARVER

World-Famous Botanist and Agricultural Inventor

by Julia Garstecki

Content Consultant
Gary R. Kremer
Executive Director
The State Historical Society of Missouri

Core Library

An Imprint of Abdo Publishing
abdopublishing.com

abdopublishing.com

Published by Abdo Publishing, a division of ABDO, PO Box 398166, Minneapolis, Minnesota 55439. Copyright © 2016 by Abdo Consulting Group, Inc. International copyrights reserved in all countries. No part of this book may be reproduced in any form without written permission from the publisher. Core Library™ is a trademark and logo of Abdo Publishing.

Printed in the United States of America, North Mankato, Minnesota
032015
092015

Cover Photo: Arthur Rothstein/US Farm Security Administration
Interior Photos: Arthur Rothstein/US Farm Security Administration, 1; Tuskegee University Archives/Museum, 4; Library of Congress, 8; Red Line Editorial, 10, 32; Tom Bean/Alamy, 12; Frances Benjamin Johnston/ Library of Congress, 16, 22, 24, 26, 43, 45; Bettmann/Corbis, 18, 38; US Department of Agriculture, 29; Corbis, 34; AP Images, 37

Editor: Jenna Gleisner
Series Designer: Becky Daum

Library of Congress Control Number: 2015931128

Cataloging-in-Publication Data
Garstecki, Julia.
 George Washington Carver: World-famous botanist and agricultural inventor / Julia Garstecki.
   p. cm. -- (Great minds of science)
Includes bibliographical references and index.
ISBN 978-1-62403-871-6
1. Carver, George Washington, 1864?-1943--Juvenile literature. 2. African American agriculturists--Biography--Juvenile literature. 3. Agriculturists-- Biography--Juvenile literature.   I. Title.
630.92--dc23
[B]   2015931128

CONTENTS

CHAPTER ONE

GROWING UP CARVER'S GEORGE

It was unlikely George Washington Carver would grow up to be an influential scientist. He was born during a time of slavery in the United States in Diamond Grove, Missouri, and was owned by Moses and Susan Carver. He was known as Carver's George. George never knew his exact birthday, but some historians believe he was born in 1864.

George Washington Carver grew up to become a notable botanist and agricultural innovator.

Little is known about George's parents. George thought his father was a slave from a nearby farm. That man was killed in an accident, and George never met him. George and his mother were kidnapped from the Carver farm shortly after George's birth. They were sold to another slave owner in Arkansas. Moses Carver hired a neighbor to find his slaves. The neighbor found only baby George. George never knew what happened to his mother.

When African people were first brought to the United States in the early 1600s, they were sold as property to white people. Many were forced to work for no pay on large farms

Poor Records

George's exact birth date is unknown because birth and death records of slaves were not well kept. Slave owners may have kept a record of the number of slaves they owned, but they often did not keep a record of their names. Slaves did not have legal rights, so legal contracts, such as marriage licenses, were also rarely kept. Because educating a slave was illegal, many were unable to read or write. Slaves could not keep records for themselves.

called plantations. On January 11, 1865, four months before the American Civil War (1861–1865) ended, Missouri slave owners legally had to emancipate, or free, their slaves. With no parents, young George and his older brother James had nowhere to go. The Carvers enjoyed the brothers and moved them from the slave cabin into their own home.

The Young Plant Doctor

George spent much of his early childhood sick with illnesses, such as whooping cough. Unable to work in the fields like his brother, he worked in the house with Mrs. Carver. Mrs. Carver also taught George how

The Civil War

Views on slavery divided the United States and sparked the Civil War. Southern states wanted to continue enslaving African Americans. The Northern states were against slavery. The issue of states' rights was another factor in the war. Southern states did not believe the government had the right to decide how people should live. They thought the laws should be determined by each state. The Civil War ended when the South surrendered on April 9, 1865.

The Carver home, which was built in 1881, still stands at the George Washington Carver National Monument in Diamond, Missouri.

to read and use garden herbs to prepare medical treatments.

Even though George played with children from other farms, he preferred to study plants. He often collected plants. He would then replant them in a garden near the Carver home. Plants that appeared sick would become healthy under his care. From a young age, George was extremely curious and loved learning.

George was also very spiritual. He believed God spoke to him through plants, flowers, rocks, and animals. This spiritual relationship often guided George through his scientific discoveries.

Finding an Education

Although slavery had been outlawed near the end of the Civil War, racism still existed. George was not allowed to learn with white children. Mrs. Carver hired George a tutor. It didn't take long for him to learn everything this tutor knew. He wanted to learn more.

When George was around 12 years old, Mrs. Carver sent him eight miles (13 km) away to Neosho, Missouri. There was a school in Neosho that welcomed African-American children. George moved in with Mariah and Andrew Watkins, an African-American couple. George and Mrs. Watkins quickly became friends through their spirituality and interest in herbs.

When George was around 13 years old, he joined the many African Americans traveling to Kansas.

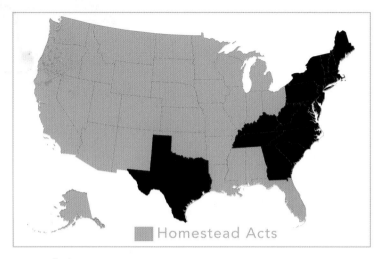

Homestead Acts

Homestead Acts

This map shows the states that took part in the Homestead Act of 1862 and later homestead acts. Abraham Lincoln signed the Homestead Act into law in 1862 to expand the United States. The act gave free land to those who claimed it. How does seeing the number of states that participated in the act help you visualize Carver's options for moving and research?

To help citizens acquire land, the US Congress had passed the Homestead Act in 1862. It provided free land where people could grow crops and make improvements. After five years, the person could own the property. Many newly-freed slaves benefitted from the Homestead Act and were able to begin new lives. George spent approximately ten years trying different jobs. Usually he worked for families doing odd jobs, such as house chores.

Around 1897 Carver wrote about the challenges he faced as a beginning scientist during his younger years:

> *Day after day I spent in the woods alone in order to collect my floral [beauties] and put them in my little garden I had hidden in brush not far from the house. . . .*

> *And many are the tears I have shed because I would break the roots or flower [off] some of my pets while removing them from the ground.*

Source: Gary R. Kremer, ed. George Washington Carver: In His Own Words. Columbia, MO: University of Missouri, 1987. Print. 20.

What's the Big Idea?

According to his reflection, how did George feel about nature from an early age? How important do you think nature was to George? What details does he include to support his main ideas?

ON THE MOVE

I n 1879, when Carver was approximately 15 years old, he enrolled in the Fort Scott Colored School in Fort Scott, Kansas. He enjoyed his studies. But one day he witnessed a violent, racist act that greatly upset him. Carver saw a group of white men murder an African-American man. Carver no longer felt safe. As a result, he dropped out of the school he loved.

The former Fort Scott Colored School still stands at the Fort Scott National Historic Site.

Segregation

The Civil War granted African Americans their freedom, but life was still difficult for them. Restaurants, movie theaters, swimming pools, and even drinking fountains were labeled to separate the races. It was difficult for African Americans to find work because few companies would hire them. Segregating schools, or separating students based on race, was ruled unconstitutional in 1954. Then in 1964 President Lyndon B. Johnson signed the Civil Rights Act, which stated it was against the law for people to be treated differently because of their race or religion.

Carver moved many times, taking odd jobs working for families. In 1884 he found a job as a desk clerk at the Union Depot train station in Kansas City, Missouri. He became friends with many white people who encouraged him to go to college. He applied to and was accepted into a small college in Highland, Kansas. But upon arriving, Carver was forced to leave. He was told that the school did not, and would not, allow African-American students.

Pursuing Science

Carver moved to Beeler, Kansas, in 1886. He tried farming his own land, but it was hard to make a living doing so. He moved again in 1889, this time to Winterset, Iowa. Here he applied for college again. This time he was welcomed at Simpson College in Iowa. Carver pursued a love of painting but switched mainly to science classes. George believed God spoke with him, helping him realize he could serve others better as a scientist.

In 1891 the Iowa State College of Agriculture and Mechanic Arts was a

Life in Beeler

While in Beeler, Carver lived and worked on a farm that he owned. He eventually built himself a house just south of Beeler, where he grew corn and vegetables. Though he was one of very few African Americans in the area, Carver formed many friendships. Settling in a new area was difficult, and as a result, people often helped each other farm and build homes. The color of Carver's skin did not matter. White townspeople included Carver in play performances and dances. He often played the accordion at these occasions.

Carver stands with a sample of soil.

leading school for agricultural education. Farming was not thought of as an academic subject before, but scientific agriculture was evolving. After so many years of growing crops, the soil was not as fertile as it once was. Farmers needed new ways of growing crops.

They asked the government for help. The government turned to universities and schools to find ways of improving agriculture. Carver's lifelong love of plants and farming was now something he could turn into a career. In 1891 Carver enrolled at Iowa State College. This decision would change his life. It would not be easy, but he was destined to become one of the best-known scientists in the country.

FURTHER EVIDENCE

Chapter Two discusses Carver's attempts to receive an education. What is the main idea of this chapter? What evidence supports it? Read more about Carver at the website below. Find a quotation about his attempts to go to college. Does the quotation support the ideas in this chapter, or does it add new information?

The Life of George Washington Carver
mycorelibrary.com/george-washington-carver

CHAPTER THREE

RESEARCHING THE PEANUT

Carver's start at Iowa State was challenging. As one of the only African-American students, he was discouraged from socializing with the white students and was even forced to eat his meals in the cafeteria basement. He struggled to find a job and pay for food and clothing. He often made his own clothing and ate wild plants and mushrooms.

Carver spent as much time as possible studying botany and horticulture.

Despite these challenges, Carver did well in school. He did best in botany and horticulture classes. These classes taught him how to grow strong and healthy plants. He also learned about cross-fertilization. This involved grafting, or joining, two different healthy plants to create new, stronger plants. Carver wrote many papers about his findings.

Cross-Fertilization

During cross-fertilization, botanists apply the pollen of a male flower to a female plant, creating a new plant. Botanists do this to create plants with particular sizes, colors, or other qualities. Carver and other scientists studied this method in hopes of growing plants that would produce more fruits and vegetables. Cross-fertilization, also known as plant hybridization, improved farmers' yields. Carver also applied cross-fertilization in hope of creating plants that could grow well in poor soil.

An Exciting Invitation

Carver graduated from Iowa State in 1896. He was offered a teaching job at the Tuskegee Institute in Alabama shortly after. Started by former slave Booker T. Washington,

Tuskegee was a new college for African-American students. Washington asked Carver to develop an agricultural program at the school. This request led Carver to feel God had chosen him to bring scientific agriculture to the South. He agreed. He would teach African-American farmers how to take care of farms. Carver was offer~

~ut botany and agriculture when he arrived in Alabama in

Becoming an Expert in the Field

Before graduating from Iowa State, Carver discussed his work with members of the Iowa Horticulture Society. They thought Carver was intelligent and hard working and had a bright future as a botanist. They encouraged him to stay at Iowa State as a graduate student. This meant he would earn another degree and become an expert in his field of study. Carver decided to stay. He was put in charge of the college's greenhouse and was given a job as a teacher. Finally he could stop working odd jobs and be a full-time scientist.

Carver, bottom center, poses for a photograph with fellow Tuskegee Institute staff members.

the fall of 1896. Unfortunately it was more difficult than he expected. At Iowa State, professors and other scientists admired his work and encouraged him to continue with experiments. At Tuskegee, other teachers were angry that Carver was paid more than they were. He also struggled to balance his teaching schedule, manage students, and perform experiments. He wanted to work on science projects of his own.

Peanut Experiments

Carver was assigned to head the Tuskegee Experiment Station. Here he could focus on projects that would help southern farmers. The soil in Alabama was worn out and unable to produce large amounts of cotton. Carver wanted to make Tuskegee a leader in southern agriculture, as well as teach southern farmers how to improve their lands.

In his experiment station, Carver grew various plants, including soybeans and peanuts. In 1896 the peanut was not a crop farmers wanted to grow. But Carver realized that cowpeas (more commonly known as black-eyed peas) and peanuts released nitrogen into the soil. Nitrogen is a gas that is a part of all living things. It is often found in fertilizer. Without it crops grow more slowly and may not produce as many fruits or vegetables.

Carver designed an experiment to see if planting peanuts would really help crops grow. His goal was to help poor farmers by growing the largest crops for the

Carver, second from right, observes his students in the Tuskegee lab.

least amount of money. In 1897 Carver began planting peanuts and cowpeas. In 1903 he observed the soil was becoming more productive. Each year the harvest was larger. Because the soil had better nutrients, healthier plants grew. Poor farmers now did not need to buy fertilizer. Carver had found a way to naturally fertilize and enrich soil. And they could grow more than just cotton. This also helped stop the South's dependence on one main crop.

The Peanut Man

From his research with peanuts, Carver learned the entire peanut could be profitable. He separated the peanut fats, oils, gums, and sugars. He explored their uses. In addition to fertilizing soil, he learned peanuts are high in protein. In addition to providing a new, cost-efficient food source, Carver's introduction of the peanut diversified people's diets by introducing a healthy food.

Carver also discovered how peanut oil could be made, using a press that broke oil cells in the peanut. Once collected, the oil could be used in salad, cooking oil, and makeup. The oils could be mixed with other chemicals to make dyes. He also looked for ways to use peanut oils to make soap and fuel. Carver became known as the Peanut Man because of the hundreds of ways he discovered to use peanuts.

CHAPTER FOUR

CONSERVATIONIST CARVER

C arver is often called the Peanut Man, but he was much more than that. Carver believed God and nature gave people everything they needed. As a conservationist, he wanted to make sure natural resources were used fully and recycled. Carver's work with the peanut is an example of this. He was dedicated to finding ways to use all of what nature had to offer. In the early 1900s,

Carver dedicated his research to developing easy and affordable methods for poor farmers.

many people in the South were poor. Carver taught people that they were in fact wealthy because God provided everything they needed to survive.

Helping Farmers

Carver could have made a lot of money by selling his discoveries and speaking to groups of people about the uses of peanuts. But according to Carver, God gave him knowledge for free, and he would share his information for the same price. Carver understood the struggles of poor African-American farmers. Racism in the South made a hard life even more difficult, and Carver wanted to help.

The Boll Weevil Invasion

In 1892 the boll weevil, a type of beetle, migrated to the United States from Mexico. This beetle infested cotton crops. Many farmers lost money because of infested crops. The boll weevil did not infest peanut or potato crops. Carver worked hard to find many uses for these crops. He helped convince farmers to grow them. Now, in addition to cotton, farmers began planting peanut and potato crops.

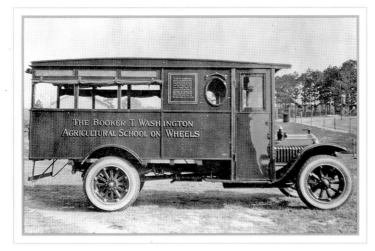

Carver's Agriculture Movable School transported equipment, recipes, and plants to farmers.

Agriculture Movable School

In 1906 Carver created the Agriculture Movable School. It was a wagon that traveled to local farms to demonstrate how to farm more successfully. To make the movable school a success, Carver partnered with Morris K. Jesup, a wealthy man who shared Carver's vision.

Jesup gave Carver enough money to create the school and supply it with equipment the farmers could use. Carver brought examples of his experiments to farmers so they could better understand what he wanted them to know. He did not charge people for his services or supplies.

Sweetening the Sweet Potato

In addition to the peanut, Carver developed many uses for the sweet potato. Like peanuts, sweet potatoes were grown easily in the poor Southern soil. They could also be stored cheaply through winter months. In 1918 a wheat shortage made it difficult to produce foods made with grain, such as bread. The sweet potato was an alternative. The US Department of Agriculture brought Carver to Washington, DC, to discuss the use of the sweet potato.

Sweet potatoes could also be turned into sugar, molasses, and chocolate or be fed to farm animals. Carver suggested the potatoes be boiled and sliced thin. Then they could be mashed and dried until they became flour. According to Carver, this was useful in breads and cakes. Carver also wrote a bulletin to teach the variety of ways the sweet potato could be stored and used. His hope was to convince people how useful the potato could be. Introducing different ways to use a new crop helped farmers maximize their own self-sufficiency and plant production. It also enforced frugal living.

Speaking at the US House Ways and Means Committee

Carver's research taught him that cotton takes nutrients from the soil, while growing peanuts puts the nutrients back in. By switching their crops, farmers could add nutrients to the soil. This is called crop rotation. This would save money because farmers would not have to buy fertilizer and their crop yields would be bigger. This idea was groundbreaking.

Helping in a Time of Need

In the late 1920s the Great Depression hit the United States. It was a time of great financial difficulty. Workers couldn't find jobs, banks lost money, and people struggled to buy food and even afford a place to live. Carver was a valuable resource during this time. He helped many people by teaching them how to use all of their available crops. He wrote newsletters and articles that taught farm families how to pickle and can foods so they would last longer. Later, even President Franklin D. Roosevelt would ask for his advice on agricultural matters.

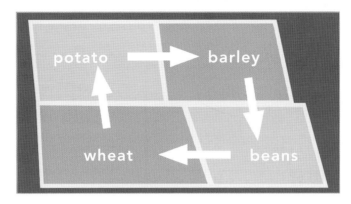

Crop Rotation

In this chapter, you read about crop rotation. This diagram shows how crop rotation works. A farm can be divided into four different sections, each planted with a different crop. Each year, the crops rotate to be planted in a different section of the farm. The different crops add different nutrients to the soil, keeping it healthy. Compare this diagram to what you have read in the text. Does this diagram help you visualize Carver's idea of crop rotation?

In 1921 Carver was asked to speak at the US House Ways and Means Committee in Washington, DC. This committee places taxes and tariffs on products. A tariff is a tax on goods coming into the United States. US farmers wanted a tariff placed on peanuts coming from other counties. This would make them more expensive, urging peanut buyers to buy cheaper, US-grown peanuts. Carver was an excellent speaker. He convinced the committee to place a tariff on peanuts.

The following text is an excerpt of Carver's speech to the US House Ways and Means Committee in 1921. He explains the importance of peanuts by describing their many uses:

> So that nothing about the peanut need to be thrown away. Here is peanut meal . . . that can be used for making flours and confections and candies, and doughnuts, and . . . ginger bread and all sorts of things of that kind.
>
> Here is a sample of peanut hearts . . . [they] must be removed from the peanut before many of the very fine articles of manufactured products can be made such as peanut butter and various confections that go into candies and so forth.
>
> Here is another thing that is quite interesting. This consists of the little skins that come off of the peanut. These skins are used for dyes. About 30 different dyes can be made from the skins. . . .

Source: Gary R. Kremer, ed. George Washington Carver: In His Own Words. Columbia, MO: University of Missouri, 1987. Print. 103–106.

Back It Up

Carver uses evidence to support his point. Write a paragraph describing the point Carver is trying to make. Then write down two or three pieces of evidence he uses to make that point.

CHAPTER FIVE

CARVER'S LEGACY

Carver's message was about using natural resources rather than human-made products. He wanted people to understand that while they might not have much money, they were not poor. Nature provided everything a person needed. This is why he devoted much of his time to finding numerous uses for different crops.

Carver continued researching until his final days.

Carver's scientific research also focused on turning agricultural products, such as peanuts, sweet potatoes, and cotton into other products, such as paint and rubber. This type of science was known as chemurgy. Today it is called biochemical engineering. Because Carver was one of the first scientists to speak about his research in this area, he is considered a pioneer of chemurgy.

Carver is also recognized for his love of nature and science. He thought the two were linked. He believed scientists should keep in mind how their research impacts the world. This was evident in his research with peanuts and sweet potatoes. To Carver they were not just crops. They were methods of enriching the soil. They could even be used in medicine and in paints that artists used.

Crossing the Color Barrier

Carver overcame many obstacles during his lifetime. For a man with such challenging beginnings, he became friends with influential people, such as Henry

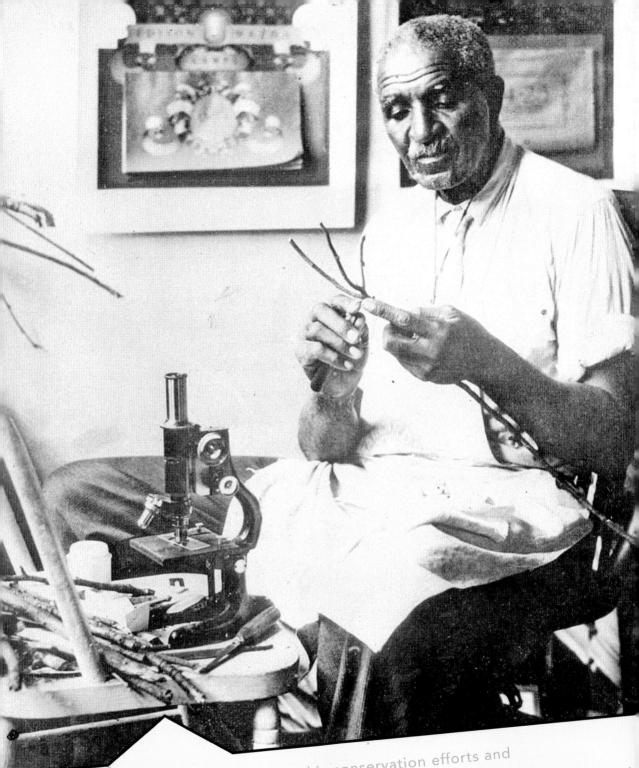

Carver is best known for his conservation efforts and finding uses for all parts of a plant.

Friend Henry Ford, right, presents Carver with a laboratory for food research in 1942.

Ford, the man who discovered more efficient methods of building cars. He spoke at many formal and important events that other African-American people were not even allowed to attend. He likely could have become very wealthy by charging for his time and services. Instead he focused on donating his time and knowledge to the poor.

George Washington Carver Foundation

Throughout the 1920s and 1930s, Carver traveled often to speak with people about his experiments. Carver continued working, even

George Washington Carver Monument

The George Washington Carver National Monument is located in Diamond, Missouri. It includes an interactive exhibit that teaches visitors about history and science. Nature trails lead to the site of his boyhood cabin. The 210-acre (85-ha) complex was funded when President Franklin D. Roosevelt dedicated $30,000 of government money to the park shortly after Carver's death in 1943. It was the first national monument dedicated to an African American.

when his health began to fail. On January 5, 1943, Carver died at the approximate age of 78.

Carver left his life savings to start the George Washington Carver Foundation. This foundation provides opportunities for African-American students to study botany and chemistry.

George Washington Carver Lives On

Whether people think of Carver as a scientist, teacher, researcher, or charitable man, he has inspired thousands of people of all races. His picture has been placed on stamps and on a half-dollar coin. Many schools are named for him. Two US military vessels are also named in his honor. He symbolizes those who desire an education and use their knowledge to improve humanity.

Ahead of His Time

Carver was far ahead of his time in terms of agricultural and conservationist ideas. During the Great Depression, he provided the United States with nutrition and more efficient ways of producing food.

Once a slave in the South, Carver's methods,

which revolutionized agriculture, ended up saving the South from economic disaster. Carver taught poor farmers to farm efficiently. By finding hundreds of uses for both peanuts and sweet potatoes, he showed people how to enrich their soil, maximize plant production, and avoid waste in a time of US hardship. Carver did not seek popularity or riches. He only sought to help others.

EXPLORE ONLINE

Carver studied chemurgy, now commonly known as biochemical engineering. Visit the website below to read about some biochemical projects scientists are doing now. Compare these current projects to the experiments of George Washington Carver.

Biochemical Engineering
mycorelibrary.com/george-washington-carver

Crop Rotation

George Washington Carver helped promote the idea of crop rotation. Crop rotation keeps the soil healthy because different plants put different nutrients into the soil. This saves farmers money because they do not need to buy as much fertilizer. Farmers and gardeners also rotate crops because it reduces the buildup of diseases. When crops are rotated, the life cycle of the disease is destroyed.

Chemurgy

Carver influenced an entirely new type of science when he took agricultural products and used them in everyday objects. For example, he discovered a way to turn peanut oil into paints and cosmetics. Because of this, he is known as a pioneer of chemurgy, which is now called biochemical engineering. Carver led this movement by speaking about the topic at various colleges, as well as to farmers. Biochemical engineers have many of the same goals Carver did, including discovering how plants can cure diseases.

Making Use of Resources

Carver strived to make use of an entire plant in a variety of
ways. He proved that expensive fertilizers or tools were not
necessary in order to use nature's products to their fullest.
Farmers could maintain healthy, productive crops with
available, natural resources.

STOP AND THINK

Say What?

Learning about Carver and botany can mean learning a lot of new vocabulary. Find five words in this book that you have never seen or heard before. Use a dictionary to find out what they mean. Rewrite the meanings in your own words. Then use each word in a new sentence.

Surprise Me

This book mentions many difficulties George Washington Carver had to overcome because of his race. After reading this book, what two or three facts about his life and the way others treated him surprised you the most? Write a few sentences about each fact, and explain why you found them surprising.

Why Do I Care?

George Washington Carver fought for the right to receive an education. While schools in the United States are now integrated, other countries still do not let certain people go to school. Why is it important to let all people have the right to an education?

You Are There

Imagine you are a poor farmer growing crops in Alabama soil. Your cotton is not growing well. Imagine George Washington Carver comes and speaks to you. What advice would he give you? What would you do? Write an essay explaining your actions.

GLOSSARY

agriculture
the science and practice of farming and improving soil for growing crops

botany
the scientific study of plants

chemurgy
the study of turning organic material into chemical and industrial materials

conservationist
a person who uses all of a natural resource so that nothing is wasted

crop rotation
the practice of growing different crops in the same space in an order that keeps the soil healthy

cross-fertilization
combining a male and female plant, sometimes of different varieties of a species, to create new or stronger plants

horticulture
the art or practice of garden management

tariff
a tax paid on an imported product

whooping cough
a contagious disease that causes severe coughing and difficult breathing

LEARN MORE

Books

Bennett, Doraine. *George Washington Carver.* Hamilton, GA: State Standards Publishing, 2012.

Marzollo, Jean. *The Little Plant Doctor: A Story about George Washington Carver.* New York: Holiday House, 2011.

Websites

To learn more about Great Minds of Science, visit **booklinks.abdopublishing.com**. These links are routinely monitored and updated to provide the most current information available.

Visit **mycorelibrary.com** for free additional tools for teachers and students.

INDEX

ABOUT THE AUTHOR

Julia Garstecki lives with her family in Bemus Point, New York. She enjoys writing books for children.